VISION ENHANCERS

How to Serve with Significance

DR. MATTHEW L. NESBITT

DR. NES INTERNATIONAL

LOS ANGELES   PASADENA

DR. MATTHEW L. NESBITT

DR. NES INTERNATIONAL
Los Angeles, CA
www.drnesintl.com

Publisher's Note:
All scriptures referenced throughout this manuscript are from the King James Version unless otherwise noted.

Ordering Information:
Quantity sales. Special discounts are available on quantity purchases by corporations, churches, associations, and others. For details, contact the Dr. Nes International at the above website.

Vision Enhancers: How to Serve with Significance/ Dr. Matthew L. Nesbitt. -- 1st ed.
ISBN 13: 978-0-9991785-0-8

Cover Design: Jayla Perry

DEDICATION

To every person whose heart to serve outweighs your desire for popularity and self-positioning, may your season manifest now!

Table of Contents

ACKNOWLEDGMENTS

I am grateful for each ministry experience that has provided unyielding wisdom to create this work. It is my hope that this books proves to be a very practical guide to your purpose in ministry and effective serving.

I am grateful for my wife, Dr. Nes, and family who remains supportive in each of my endeavors.

INTRODUCTION

In America, individuality and self-sufficiency are notable hallmarks in our culture. Today, there are a plethora of books and resources on shelves across the country that focus on individual development, self-empowerment, or even *self*-help. Much of what we do, our goals, our pursuits, our desires center on "self." Everybody seems to be chasing *their* dreams and most often become intoxicated with the idea of "getting theirs". Many are on the quest to make things happen for themselves. But many fail to understand that their purpose in the earth cannot be fully achieved by individual effort; it must come through the use of a multitude of individuals who have been specifically assigned to one's life to assist in the acquisition of purposeful living.

3

Habbakuk 2:2 says "And the LORD answered me, and said, Write the vision, and make it plain upon tables, so he may run that reads it." Notice in this verse that there is a visionary who writes the vision, and there are runners who run with the vision. This book is focused on the runners: those who have been called to serve and to assist in another man's vision. In this book, you will be enlightened on ways to move from sitting and merely being "a part" of a church to being a vital contributor and an asset to the ministry. This book further illuminates how to utilize the gifts, talents, and abilities that God gave you to ultimately bless and enhance the vision of your leader. It will also address various pitfalls and enemies to your assignment and show you how to stay focused when serving in ministry. Lastly, this book will highlight the blessings of those who have been called to serve the vision!

If your goal is to take your serving to the next level and your heart's burden is to be a tremendous blessing to your leader, this book is for you! This book has been written and packed with practical yet potent tools to empower you to be the best runner you can be! Your eyes will open to your assignment as a

Vision Enhancer, as God will position you in a place to assist in turning your leader's vision into a reality!

DR. MATTHEW L. NESBITT

1

UNDERSTANDING THE VISION

In the bible, Habbakuk 2:2 says "And the LORD answered me, and said, Write the vision, and make it plain upon tables, so he may run that reads it." There are some very important insights in this scripture that show us key characteristics of leaders with a vision and of those who are assigned to assist as runners of the vision.

The role of the leader is to receive the God-given vision. This vision must then be made plain and translated so those who are called to be a part of the vision can run with it. It becomes your role as the runner of the vision to fully understand the vision of your leader so that you can effectively run with what's been translated. Many of us might receive a small portion of what we think the vision entails, but have

7

failed to gain a full understanding of the vision. This can cause us to be ineffective in our ability to fully serve and run with the vision. So how do you come to understand the vision of your leader?

3 Ways to Understand the Vision of Your Leader:

1. <u>Learn about your Leader and Ministry</u>

This is especially important when connecting to a new ministry, where you are fully knowledgeable of the vision. You may have recently joined the church and are considered a new member, or you might have been a part of the church for many years and had little involvement. Many churches now have New Members class or some type of orientation to provide you information about the ministry, your leaders, salvation, and other Biblical truths that are helpful for one's Christian foundation. And I know it might seem overwhelming or appear boring to be required to take a 4-week (or longer) course, but this will be very helpful to your development as a Vision Enhancer! Often this is a great way to discover some of the basic tenets of the ministry and your leaders, from their history to the types of programming and overall culture of the church!

This is very important because God gives every leader a different ministry focus and assignment for their local church. Although, the focus of every vision should be centered on discipleship (which is found within the *Great Commission* in Matthew 28:19), each leader will have a different method or approach that is used to spread the Gospel in their specific region. This is often based upon their own spiritual DNA, which is how God has wired them through their gifting, talents, abilities, and personality. Some leaders' visions are more focused on youth and touching the next generation; others are focused more on simply teaching and educating the Body; others are strongly focused on music and arts, using this as a tool for edification and evangelism; others' ministries might have a focus on the community at large and spend time on outreach that impacts various populations within the surrounding community.

Perform your due diligence and learn as much as you can about where you are planted, as it will be vital in your ability to serve and grow!

2. Meet with your Pastor or Senior leadership staff

Once you have taken advantage of the New Members class, orientation, or other avenues to learn more about the vision of the church, it is often helpful to set a meeting time with the Pastor or Senior Staff. This is an opportunity to make the connection physically and hear some of the things from the heart of that(those) leader(s). Romans 10:17 talks about how faith comes by hearing! Sitting at the table and hearing your leader express their heart and some of the things that God has given them carries much value. It acts as a vision download and will activate the faith needed to accomplish the vision! Ask yourself, When was the last time I scheduled a meeting with my Pastor or leadership staff? This is not a meeting where you come into the office with a problem, needing counsel, nor making any request; this is a time to just sit and hear the heartbeat of your leader's vision to ensure that you are fully aligned. This is a time to hear your leader talk about where the ministry is going, the plans and the focus for the year or season, where the ministry is headed and the direction it's going—this is a time to discuss their vision and the various strategies they deem essential for its fulfillment.

The Vision Enhancer goes the extra mile to ensure that they understand the heart of their leader and that they locate the heartbeat of the vision. In John 13:23, Jesus was talking to his disciples and sharing some vital information. There was one, John (the beloved), that came in closer and leaned on Jesus' bosom. It allowed him to gain further insight and clarity from Jesus, while the other disciples were too far away to receive. Make the connection and set a time to receive a vision download!

3. Remain Prayerful

Understanding your leader's vision and aligning to become a runner of the vision is highly spiritual. Why is it spiritual? Firstly, because God has released a vision and an assignment in the earth to your leader, and the enemy doesn't want it to ever manifest. Ephesians 6:12 says, "For we wrestle not against flesh and blood, but against principalities, against powers, against the rulers of the darkness of this world, against spiritual wickedness in high places." The enemy knows that the vision is going to bring change to your city or region and that countless souls that will be saved, encouraged, healed, and delivered through its fulfillment. So, he wages a war to keep the visionary from translating the vision to the runners, and he keeps the runners inactive so they never run with the vision that has been released, effectively halting the process of fulfillment.

One of tools that the enemy will use is to keep you from fully understanding the vision of your leader. Since the vision carries spiritual weight, it cannot be received in the natural. 1 Corinthians 2:14 (NIV) says, "The person without the Spirit does not accept the things that come from the Spirit of God but considers them foolishness, and cannot understand them because they are discerned only through the Spirit." Some of you might be saying, "Well, I just don't understand why the Pastor keeps talking about getting more space and acquiring another building? I don't know why the Pastor has such a focus on missions and giving all this stuff away to people in need. We could definitely use that money for something else! Why does Pastor keep focusing on these kids and youth?" These are only examples of some of the questions and concerns that arise and the confusion that comes from not having a complete understanding. You won't ever understand the vision in your flesh! It makes no sense to your humanity and requires prayer and you asking God to reveal His greater purpose so that you can embrace what God is doing through the set man! *Remember, this is not your Pastor's vision, but this is the vision that God gave your Pastor!*

When you begin to pray and ask God to further reveal the vision to you, He opens your spiritual understanding. Ephesians 1:18 explains how we are to effectively perceive: "The eyes of your understanding being enlightened; that ye may know what is the hope of his calling..." Not with your natural eyes, but with a different set of eyes—your spiritual eyes, the eyes of your understanding! The Vision Enhancer's prayer is not to see in the natural but to perceive things in the spirit.

2

DEVELOPING WITHIN THE VISION

The God-given vision that your leader has is entirely too big for them to complete alone! That is the reason why God assigns certain individuals like yourself to come alongside their leader and be the runners of the vision. They exercise faith and work in the earth to ensure that the vision comes to pass, because we know that faith without works is dead! We see this example in Exodus 18 with Moses. Moses was taught a very valuable lesson from his father-in-law, Jethro. He advised Moses that he was taking on too much and had too many responsibilities. He advised him to appoint those who could assist him in carrying the load of ministry. But notice that Moses did not go out and just select random people; he selected honorable men who could handle the delegated authority to run with the vision.

Jesus needed runners as well! The vision and the goal was to get this gospel around the world to all men, sharing the message of Jesus Christ. He chose 12 disciples to mentor and train for 3 ½ years who would, after His death, birth the church and carry the gospel around the world, making new disciples. Jesus could not do it alone, and your Pastor cannot do it alone either!

One of the major challenges of those who serve in the local church is understanding how everything works together. Once you have been ignited with the vision and have gained an understanding of your leader's heart, you'll need some insights on where to start running.

Many questions arise:

- How do I assist my leader in fulfilling their vision?
- In which area should I serve?
- How can I be most effective in blessing my local church?
- How do I get started, once I understand the vision?
- How does this align with my own vision?

Let's uncover how to develop a vision within the larger scope of your leader's vision!

Personal Vision

The Vision Enhancer must come to the place of totally embracing who God has created them to be. This is the identification and acknowledgement of how you were wired! God uniquely created each of us with a distinct set of gifts, skills, and abilities in order to accomplish our purpose in the earth. You must ask yourself some very critical questions. For example: What do I do well? What are my strengths *and* weaknesses? What are my gifts? What talents do I possess? These are often the tools and the mix of gifts needed to execute fully the different areas of vision (personal, professional, pastoral).

Everyone should have a personal vision for their lives! One's vision is a mental picture of what you see in the totality of your life. It is a God-given concept which is typically connected to your purpose in the earth. It is something you wake up thinking about. It is connected to your passion. You've envisioned it. You see it vividly. This is something that you see coming to pass in the future, that is going to require your hard work and dedication.

I want to layout the below scenario:

You have a degree in business and finance and are currently working in the banking industry. You are growing in management and have really honed your skill set within the scope of leadership and banking. Although this might be your professional job, you are also very passionate about homelessness. You have a heart for those who are out on the streets for various reasons and who may have fallen on hard times. You have a dream of opening a homeless shelter in your city. You've envisioned getting a grant to run a facility with 150 beds. Here, entire families can stay and receive resources and assistance, ultimately transitioning them into a permanent place of residence. Ever since you were 5 years old, you saw homeless people and felt a need to do something that would impact them on a larger scale. You have kept abreast regarding the latest data and trends. You have even conducted research on the development of facilities and the process it takes to serve the homeless community. Although you do not have the resources and connections to make it happen right now, you have the faith to see this vision come to pass one day.

Pastor's Vision

As you are gearing up to be a Vision Enhancer and run effectively with the vision of your leader, there are some distinctions that must first be made.

Your Personal vision is NOT the same as your Pastor's vision

Don't make the mistake and believe that your personal or professional vision is the same as your leader's vision for the local church. Although there might be a similar passion, and goals may overlap, God has given your pastor a vision and assignment that is different from your own. Do not make the mistake of trying to push YOUR vision upon the pastor, while neglecting the vision that God has given him. Perhaps God has given your pastor a detailed vision within the context of Missions and Evangelism to low-income and gang-infested communities within the city. Just because your Pastor is not directly assisting the homeless(your passion), you cannot take on the mindset that he is not sensitive to homeless communities or that he doesn't show any interest in or has not done anything outside of low-income and gang-infested communities. Do not make the mistake of thinking, "He is not passionate about helping people less fortune than him and I'm not certain I belong at this ministry."

All of these, would be incorrect assumptions and examples of how your personal vision tries to infiltrate your pastor's vision. Remember, you have been called to the local church, not to push your own agenda and vision, but that of your leader.

Pushing your vision and neglecting the pastor's vision is a great way to cause DI-VISION.

Learn to rehearse the pastor's vision and not your own!

Your local church should not be used a platform to promote your professional vision.

Again, the local church should not be used as a place to push your own vision, nor is it the platform for personal or professional vision. God has put something very powerful in you, whether that is a gifting in ministry, business, or influence in some other area of life. But this does not mean that you can neglect the Pastor's vision and use the local church as your own platform. I have witnessed countless individuals bring their professional visions to church, push the agenda of their business or organization, and want the church to immediately buy in and evolve around everything that *they* do. I have also seen musically or artistically talented people refuse to be a part of the Pastor's vision for the local church music department; instead they only wanted to be used when the opportunity arose to be in the spotlight.

However, the local church is NOT your platform to push your own agenda or a way to gain influence and support from those who attend the ministry. The local church is a place where people worship and gather, become empowered by the Word, and are trained to disciple others; they then become the runners of their leader's vision to touch lives for the Lord.

How to Develop Vision within the Vision

Now that we have distinguished the types of vision, let's focus on gaining an understanding of how to create vision within your Pastor's vision. We will gain clarity on how to be effective as a Vision Enhancer and become a key asset to the vision.

This happens in three distinct ways:

1. <u>Opened Eyes</u>

In 2 Kings 6, Elisha had a servant who was assisting him at a very critical time in his ministry. They arose and it appeared that the Syrian Troops had surrounded them and that their lives were in danger. In verse 17, Elisha prays a powerful prayer: "And Elisha prayed, and said, LORD, I pray thee, open his eyes, that he may see. And the LORD opened the eyes of the young man; and he saw: and, behold, the mountain *was* full of horses and chariots of fire round about Elisha." Once the servant's eyes were opened, he stopped seeing from his own perspective and was able to see out of the lenses of his leader— and he saw victory!

If you are going to develop a vision within a vision, you cannot look out of your scope and your vision. Instead you must pray that God opens your eyes so that you can see what your leader sees. This causes you to put your agenda down, put your ideologies away, and truly get in a place where you take on the spirit to serve. You come to terms with the vision that God has given your leader: My Pastor has a vision for youths and that is not going to change. My leader has a heart for Evangelism and he wants everybody on board for Outreach every week. My Pastor has a vision for a larger multi-purpose facility and wants to buy other properties in the area to affect our immediate neighborhood. Settle it! This is the Pastor's heart and vision, and this is where the ministry is pushing!

No longer is it about your agenda and what you believe, but it becomes all about the vision that God has given your Pastor, and you are positioned in a place to see what they see!

Although God has anointed you to become a powerful leader, you must first have the grace of a humble servant. "But he that is the greatest among you shall be your servant." (Matthew 23:11). This requires taking on a different perspective. You are not at the ministry to display all your gifts; you are not at your church to run things or be the boss; you are not at the church to have everything your way or it's the highway. God has called you there to take on the heart of your leader, see it from where God has given it to him, and take the posture of a servant! The first step to developing vision within your leader's vision is to see from a different perspective: seeing the vision as God has given it to him.

23

2. Identify the Missing Parts

In 1 Corinthians 12, Paul gives us an analogy of the Body and how it is comprised of many parts. He talks about how there is one body, but there are many parts. He also discusses the significance of each part of the body and how the foot cannot say that there is no need for the hand, and how the ear cannot say that there is no need for the eyes. Although they are different parts of the entity, they all carry some significance to the totality of the body!

In order for the vision to be fully functioning, it needs all of its parts in motion and operating. This means there must be skillful people who are assigned to the vision and who are serving in various capacities in the church. Some have the misconception that their Pastor can do everything, and that since the Lord gave him the vision, he must have the gifts, talents, and abilities to make things happen. But that's not true! The leader might have a certain skill set and can assist in the work, but that's not his primary responsibility. His primary responsibility is to vision-cast and translate the vision so that runners are infused with the direction and heart to assist in carrying it out!

The Vision Enhancer identifies body parts within the vision that are not functioning.

There may be areas within the ministry that simply have not been activated, or there may be areas where there is no one in place to initiate that component. These areas are a part of the vision, but no one has stepped up to serve or to take on leadership capacity.

Your Pastor might have a vision to utilize grants and other funding to develop an extensive youth program. Although he is imbued with ideas for youth programming and has an extensive vision for what it will entail, he may have no experience writing grants or have limited experience with outside sources of funding.

The Vision Enhancer identifies areas in the ministry that need strengthening or support.

Your Pastor might have the desire to launch the singles ministry in the church; everyone is excited about it and a few have even volunteered to help. But you find that there is no one to head this area or provide structure and programming for it. You identify that area and understand that if this ministry had some support or strengthening it would be a vital ministry of the church.

.

3. Work It

Okay, so you are seeing the vision through the eyes of your leader and you have identified some missing parts. What's next?

The Vision Enhancer must now see their Pastor's vision and form vision within the set vision.

Now, you have an understanding of the larger vision (Pastor's vision); you understand that your serving has nothing to do with pushing your own personal or professional vision. But, you will discover that some of the gifts, talents, and abilities that fuel your personal and professional visions can be used to serve in the local church. The Bible talks about how your gift will make room for you! Some of your innate passions and skills, when used in the local church, can provide structure and leadership to some given areas. This means taking a component of your leader's larger vision and allowing God to give you insights on how to further develop and birth that area. It places you in the position of becoming an answer to your leader's prayer, and manifests into a strong runner who serves the vision.

Some of you reading this book might have a strong passion for education and enjoy working with children. You might be a natural educator within the scope of the school system or you may even operate your own daycare. You hear the announcement that the youth programming needs volunteers to help in serving the children of your church. A lightbulb should trigger in you, and you should immediately start discovering the areas of need. You begin to learn about the programming and your eyes begin to envision the things that would enhance this ministry. You are gaining vision within the vision! Remember you are just not serving, but you have been called to serve with significance! Get a vision to take that area to the next level and move from being a liability to a vital asset!

You might teach children Monday through Friday within the school system, and are also highly skilled in the development of relevant and effective lesson plans. This might lead to a desire in assisting with the development of curriculum and activities for the various age-specific classrooms at the church! You might even have the opportunity to meet with the director and staff and provide them with some essential strategies that you learned in your educational training to become a teacher. Or you might want to consider being included in the rotation schedule of teachers and volunteering a few times a month. Although this might not be in direct correlation to your personal or professional vision, you are positioning yourself in the local church to bless the body by becoming a runner of the larger vision.

Everything you need is in YOU!

God has custom-designed you with everything that you need to be a blessing to your leader and serve the vision. Sitting and watching others is no longer an option; feeling like you are not needed is no longer an option; waiting for someone to find you to get your hands busy working is no longer an option. The

Bible says in Ecclesiastes 9:10 (NIV), "Whatever your hand finds to do, do it with all your might...." No serving is too small, even if you are behind the scenes and serving where no one sees you. You might be in the sound and audio booth, or cleaning the church when everyone else leaves, or writing the grants for the ministry. Or you might be in a place where you are seen by everyone. Whatever level or capacity you occupy, serve the vision as unto the Lord!

Serving and having vision within the vision is going to require an investment on three levels (3 T's):

Time

If you are really going to be effective in serving the vision and are committed to becoming a Vision Enhancer, it is going to require your time. This can be one of the major drawbacks for many, causing them to never move from the place of sitting into the position of running. Serving and running with the vision of your leader is going to take some of your time, whether that is time planning; writing; working; or developing strategies. Overall, there is a necessary time commitment where you will need to expend mental and physical energies to be effective.

Talent

We all have been gifted by God with certain talents. We can learn some essential lessons from the parable of the talents in the Gospel of Matthew. All of them used their talents except one of them who decided to bury and hide his talent. Too many of us are not utilizing the very talent that God has given us! It was never meant to be sat on, hidden, or buried; it was meant to be sown and invested so that it would yield increase. The Vision Enhancer knows his talents and abilities and has no problem using them to serve his leader's vision. He realizes that they are not his to begin with, but they were given by God.

Treasure

God is our source, but He provides us with various resources in the earth to further the vision. A Vision Enhancer is always looking for ways to be a blessing to his ministry. You might have a job or career where you make a substantial amount of money, and your tithes and offerings can be great fuel for the vision. You also might have access to various social or business networks that can be a blessing to your leader's vision, from those who are carpenters or builders who can provide various labor services to the church, to business owners who would love to donate monies or their resources to expand the reach of your church within the community. Vision Enhancers understand that God is the source, and He provides us with various resources in the earth; they have the heart and hand to release those resources to further the vision! "For where your treasure is, there will your heart be also" (Matthew 6:21 KJV).

DR. MATTHEW L. NESBITT

3

CHARACTERISTIC OF A VISION ENHANCER

What qualities should the Vision Enhancer possess? What are the characteristics of those who are called to run with the vision of their leader? Next, I want to provide you with vital character traits needed to be an effective Vision Enhancer.

Owners vs. Renters Mentality

Over the years I have seen some very distinct differences between owners and renters. Whether it be a house or a car, there are certain characteristics and mindsets that individuals take on when placed in both positions. I want to use this analogy of the owner and renter to provide some of the characteristics of an effective Vision Enhancer.

When you make the investment to purchase a house, it is totally different from renting. When renting, you might have to pass a credit check, provide previous rental history, show proof of income and put down a deposit. But, when you want to purchase a house, there is a much larger investment with a bank involved and a significantly higher amount of money needed to acquire the property. You'll discover that lots of people will rent, but not everyone wants or are in a position to buy. Why? Many times it's because of the capacity of the investment.

If you are going to be an effective runner of the vision the first thing that you must do is BUY into it! In many churches, you will find a lot of people who sit in the pews and never move from being a renter to an owner of the vision. They may have plans to move soon or might be in transition where they have no plans to stay for an extended time. Renting for many people is a safer option that offers less responsibility and more convenience. Here are three examples of a Renter's Mentality:

1. "Theirs" vs. "Ours"

When my wife and I first got married we rented our first house. After living there for some months there were a few things that started going wrong. Before I started to look for solutions or fix the things myself, I would often tell my wife, "Let's call the owner because that is not our responsibility." I was reluctant to do anything extra, because after all, this was not *our* house; it was the landlord's.

This is similar to your Pastor's vision. If a problem comes up or something is not working well, we have the tendency to blame everything on the Pastor. "That's what the Pastor wanted to do." "I don't know what they're doing down at that church." You are a part of the vision, but act as if everything is "theirs" and not "yours." Many take on the mindset of "theirs" and never get to the place of taking ownership and buying in to the idea that the ministry is "ours." You, as the Vision Enhancer, must get to the place where you accept it, buy in to the vision, and take ownership. It's not your role to throw everything on everybody else. The Vision Enhancer takes initiative and shares the load of the vision with your leader. Vision Enhancers always affirm their leader and remind them that they are in this together. In essence, they have fully bought in to the vision God has given.

2. Short-Term Stays

When my wife and I were renting the places where we lived, it often was an indication that it was for a short-term stay. We were at earlier stages in life and marriage and were not certain about our final placement and therefore was not ready to make a full commitment to purchase. Hence, we moved frequently, as our family grew rapidly.

One of the worst things that you can tell a Pastor is, "I don't know how long I am going to be at the church." Or, "I am just here for a season; when my season is up I will have to leave." Of course, there are various reasons and each case is different, but generally this is an indication of a renter's mentality. You'll see a vicious cycle within the church of people coming and people leaving. When there is no stability within the congregation or leadership team, it becomes very difficult to build consistency. ***When you are called to support the vision of your leader it is important to first unpack and get settled.*** Some sway back and forth trying to decide if they should be at the ministry or if they should they stay or should they back up and recant the decision to serve and run with the vision. The Bible says in James 1:8 that "a double minded man is unstable in all of his ways!" Make the decision to totally buy into the vision of your leader and make the commitment and responsibility necessary to be used to further what God has called him to do.

3. Not Focused on Improvement

I rented a car several times in the last year and have noticed a pattern each time I returned it. I find that I never take it to the car wash to spray it off or clean it up before I returned it, and that I am totally fine leaving it in worse condition than when I first got it! Ask yourself, when is the last time you washed a rented car?!

Renters are often not concerned about something devaluing and are least concerned about increasing its value. At your church, you might be witnessing some areas of the ministry that need strengthening or support. As a Vision Enhancer who has taken on the mindset of an owner, you don't overlook these areas, but you seek ways to enhance and improve their functionality. You look out of a different set of eyes! If you see paper on the floor, you pick it up; if there is a need for volunteers, you are the first to sign up; if your leader needs pledges for a project, you are the first to make the donation.

Take ownership!

After a renter moves out of their home, the home does not typically gain value unless renovations are made. Oft times, repairs are needed. Why? Because as renter you are often not concerned about upgrades or major improvements to the house. But any good owner that knows about the power of their investment understands that they must make continuous improvements—improvements to the flooring, cabinetry, bathrooms, etc. This prevents the home from losing its value and creates home equity, causing the property to have more value than when originally purchased! *The Vision Enhancer wants to ensure that his service has significance and that the value and components of the ministry have enhanced since he decided to run with the vision. Your role is to add value!*

Solution Driven

As you work closer and closer to your leader and have a more microscopic view of the vision, you will come across problems. That's right, there WILL be problems! Whether these problems crop up in the developmental stages of the ministry or in the stages of growth and expansion, there will be times when you are serving the vision when a seemingly challenging reality might be faced. We see this example biblically in the book of Numbers where Moses sent 12 spies into the land of Canaan to research and to give more information about the land. There are some valuable lessons that we can learn from this example when setting out to perform a task on behalf of your leader.

In Numbers 13, ten of the spies missed some insightful points about serving another man's vision.

The Vision Enhancer never questions IF it can be done, but provides insights on HOW it can be done!

They forgot that the Lord already told Joshua that the land was theirs despite any of the opposition they would face. Your leader might have the vision to feed the needy, and request that you gather information and research programs and organizations within the community which can assist in achieving this goal. God has given him this component of the vision and it has to happen! So, you must move from the place of IF and into the place of HOW. You might start talking with churches or organization that are already successful in this venture; you might reach out to the local food bank; you might get on the internet and research how your church's nonprofit status can help you achieve this goal within the ministry! When you are serving your leader's vision, settle the IF and become resourceful; be the refreshing voice that brings back the HOW.

The Vision Enhancer is mature, he limits negativity the comes to the ears of their leader.

Listen, your Pastor already hears enough negativity; the last thing that they need is someone running with the vision that always has something negative to say. They are excited and trying to rally and ignite everyone around the vision, and you are saying "I wouldn't do it this way, Pastor" or, "I think that might be too much for us" … "It will take us a long time to get that done" … "I don't think they will let us do that." You have not been called to feed your Pastor's ears with negativity, but you have been placed in his life to echo and support all that is in his heart to do. You have to learn how to hold your tongue, even if you are in the process of supporting the vision and can't see it yourself. John 6:63 says "…the words that I speak unto you, they are spirit, and they are life." Go and pray and exhaust all your options, before releasing the spirits of doubt, faithlessness, and negativity in the atmosphere. Stop finding so many problems, and start uncovering the solutions!

In Numbers 13:30, Caleb and Joshua were the two out of the 12 who silenced the people's negativity and said to their leader, "Moses, we can do it!" Despite what the majority believed about the limitations of the land and the power of the giants it possessed, those two had faith like their leader and the faith of God to possess the promise!

Displays Loyalty

We live in a generation now that does not seem to value the character trait of loyalty. When God connects you with a ministry and you begin to serve your leader, one of the most valuable traits that you can possess is that of loyalty. It always amazing me how excited people are when they first connect with a ministry—excited, motivated, and so thankful that the Lord has brought them there. They might even tell the Pastor, "The Lord sent me here!" They are moved to participate in ministry and utilize their gifting and talents to be a blessing to church. But after some time has passed, their very zeal and commitment to their ministry is tested. The excitement that they entered the doors with is now being questioned; they now are contemplating whether this is the placed God has really called them to be. *A Vision Enhancer has the maturity to understand that their loyalty will be tested at many points while serving, but they must possess the Spirit of God to stay aligned and focused on the purpose of their placement.*

I want to use the Biblical example of Noah and his sons to highlight character traits necessary for those who are called to enhance the vision of their leader.

In Genesis 9:18-28, we are given a detailed account of Noah and his three sons: Shem, Ham, and Japheth. The Bible says in verse 21 that Noah drank of the wine in the vineyard and became drunken. Now, I will not take the time to dive into the debate on whether drinking is a sin or not...but I will point out that Noah was in rare form!

As a Vision Enhancer who is working alongside the vision of another, you will have opportunities to work more closely with your leader. This often requires meetings, conferences, strategy sessions, and spending time together working in your designated area. There will be lots of time spent where you see them as a real human and not just a spiritual leader! Most people just get to see them in the pulpit preaching or teaching, but as you serve you get to see a more detailed picture of their day-to-day life.

A Vision Enhancer doesn't reveal their leader's weaknesses.

Let me share something with you: your leader has weaknesses too! Yes, I said it! They are not totally developed or skillful in *all* areas of the ministry. I know many prolific preachers who are amazing speakers in the pulpit, but who are horrible planners. I know other leaders who are great at speaking and love having the microphone, but when you ask them to write a letter, that eloquent speech is unapparent! Working closely in ministry you are going to see weaknesses in your leader and in other people with whom you are serving. You might be working with your leader, trying to get a grant completed to initiate a program that revolutionizes the effectiveness of your ministry. You might be waiting on feedback from your leader so that you can complete the necessary requirements and find out that they are clueless on how to provide an analysis of the problems that persist in the community. Your leader might not come out and tell you, but you notice the verbiage needed to effectively position the ministry is not up to the standards. This does not give you license to embarrass or share about your Pastor's weakness or inferiority in this area, saying, "He just doesn't know what he is doing," or, "They just do not have their stuff together," or saying, "I love my church, but they are just unprofessional!" Like you, your Pastor is not supposed to be good at everything! Why are you there??? *Vision Enhancers can pick up on weaknesses within their leader/ministry and use their skill set to strengthen these areas, causing them to excel!* The Vision Enhancer constantly speaks well of his ministry and leader to others and always illuminates their strengths!

A Vision Enhancer knows what to keep in the house.

In Genesis 9:21, the story goes on to explain how Noah was drunk and naked inside his tent. One of the sons (Ham) saw him inside and immediately went outside to share the information to his brothers (Shem and Japheth). Instead of helping and covering his father, he decided to take what he saw inside of the tent to the outside of the tent.

The older generation used to say often, "What happens in this house, stays in this house." What they were saying was that everyone on the outside does not need to know EVERYTHING about what's going on inside. While serving you might see things, hear things, or even experience things that you might not totally understand or agree with but it's not your role as the Vision Enhancer to become disloyal and share things with those who are not in the intimate space that you possess. You should never leave a meeting and share information to those who are not a part of that space. For example, if you are a Minister or leader in your church, you should not share your disgruntlement to a church member. This is can be very disloyal. Some people have made judgements about your ministry or leader and have never stepped foot inside or visited; they are outside, just as Noah's two sons. But because people have brought them information from the inside to the outside, seeds of discord and disloyalty have been sown.

Vision Enhancers must understand that their loyalty will be most often tested when they are in their FEELINGS! That's right…when you are feeling some kinda way! It is here where you have to decide whether to move past your feelings and remain loyal to the place God has called you or choose to unload and dump them on everyone with whom you come into contact. This typically occurs during these two instances:

1. Handling Disagreements

When you have been called to serve your leader, you are not going to agree about everything. There will be times when you simply are opposed to a decision or direction of the vision and you are not seeing eye to eye. You will have the choice of whether to remain faithful and submitted, while displaying loyalty and commitment through the disagreement. Vision Enhancers refuse to air everything to others who are not members or even a part of the ministry. You must have the maturity to stay loyal and still speak well of your leader. Your disagreement does not deny the call or vision.

2. Handling Being Corrected (Rebuked)

There will be times when your leader must bring correction, change of direction, or a rebuke. This is prime time for you to get in your feelings! You may be tempted to leave the church and drive off mad, hurt, and misunderstood. At this time, you have the opportunity to point out all of weaknesses of the church and what you deem wrong with your leader and their leadership style. Since you have been rebuked, you feel justified to throw your leader and the ministry under the bus because you feel you have been put "out there." The Vision Enhancer must stop, pray, and remain loyal despite how they feel after correction or rebuke.

A Vision Enhancer guards and protects their leader/ministry at all cost.

In Genesis 9:23, the Bible talks about how the two other sons (Shem and Japheth) went backwards in the room and laid a garment over their father to cover his nakedness. Later we learn that the son who went out of the tent and did not cover their father, was cursed and that the two brothers who covered him with a garment, were blessed.

Just because you see areas of the ministry or your leader uncovered does not mean that everyone needs to know. I grew up around many of the older saints in the church. It was always amazing to me how they might not have done everything right, but if they were a part of a church, they truly loved their Pastor! Baby, they would fight you, cut you, and maybe even run to the trunk to shoot you if you spoke negatively about their Pastor. They understood that their leader made mistakes; they were not perfect and neither was their church. But they recognized that the Pastor was God's man, and they understood the principles of loyalty and covering where God had planted them. Many of these faithful ones were loyal to their churches for many years and lived long, prosperous lives!

Vision Enhancers guard their leaders at all costs and understand the Scripture when it speaks of not giving any room to the enemy (Ephesians 4:27).

Maximizes Influence

Influence, according to Dictonary.com, is "the capacity to have an effect on the character, development, or behavior of someone or something, or the effect itself." Vision Enhancers understand the power of their presence and how this, in turn, affects everyone that is connected to the vision. And many of you might be saying, "I am only an Usher/Greeter...I only assist with childcare on Sunday mornings once a month. I serve on the camera or audio team. I merely help with security and parking." God hasn't merely called you to these areas to take up space or to fill a spot; He has called you there so that you can display the character of Christ and make a positive influence on the ministry. There are three major components necessary to positively maximize your influence in the area where you serve.

1. <u>Value the Culture</u>

Every church has a culture. What is the culture of your church? One of the best ways to understand culture is the statement, "This is how we do things here." Believe it or not, culture is the strongest force in any church or organization. You can walk into many churches and immediately pick up on the culture of that ministry. Some churches have a culture of love and fellowship, where as soon as you hit the grounds of the church it is sensed and felt. You feel it from the parking lot attendant, to the greeters at the doors, to the people inside the church; they are extremely inviting and the atmosphere is full of love and kindness or not. They also might stress the importance of "community" within the church and facilitate social outlets such as small groups or fellowships. Other ministries might have a strong culture of Praise and Worship. They strive to set an atmosphere to encourage a personal relationship with God through the corporate expression of praise and worship. Individuals might lay prostrate on the floor, or express praise through a shout or dance. Other ministries have a culture of wealth and prosperity, where others have a culture of education and equipping. It is important to know that no church is the same.

Culture is created at the top, with your leader, and sustains all other levels of the church.

The vision is so important because this is how God gave it to the leader, and it trickles down to the people. So, I'll ask you again, what is the culture of your church? A Vision Enhancer takes time to understand the culture of his church, actively engages in the culture, and promotes it to others within his sphere.

If you know that the culture of your house is to be equipped with biblical knowledge and learning, why don't you attend Bible study?! Why aren't you taking advantage of the ministry offerings that promote growing in the Word? Remember, the culture is "how we do things here!" Your role as a Vision Enhancer is to engage with the Body and come into alignment with the vision of the house. So, if the culture of your church is strong Praise and Worship, why are you just looking around or sitting during these times? I have heard people say, "I just don't do all of that." Well, if you are going to be a vital part of your ministry and come into alignment with the vision, you must drop your individual mindset and come into the power of unity. When everyone is on one accord, this is when the power of God is released!

2. Ignite Others

Vision Enhancers understand that they have the power to ignite others by their presence! There might be others within the ministry who have a bad attitude. These individuals are unwilling to follow directions and at times are difficult to deal with. But, when these individuals come into contact with the God on the inside of you, they cannot help but be positively influenced by the fire and love for ministry that you possess!

Vision Enhancers are NOT thermometers but thermostats.

As a Vision Enhancer, you have not been called to serve the vision and adjust to the temperature of others, but you understand the importance of climates and atmospheres; you become a temperature-setter! Never adjust yourself or lower your standard of excellence to accommodate others who do not have the heart or vision of your leader.

If you are a greeter, you do not succumb to the people whom you are greeting; they might have had a horrible morning and all kinds of negative things going on at home. As soon as you see them coming, it is your role to give them a hug that is laced with love and encouragement; this might be the strength needed for them to worship God, removing the burden they came with! The Spirit of God goes from heart to heart and from breast to breast! You become a flame keeper and ensure that everyone who encounters you encounters the presence of God. Matthew 5:16 says, "Let your light so shine before men, that they may see your good works, and glorify your Father which is in heaven."

Vision Enhancers who have learned the art of igniting others possess three important qualities:

1. They possess God's Love
2. They are genuine
3. They are consistent

You will quickly learn that you cannot ignite others in your own strength. If you try it on your own, you will become frustrated, irritated, and lose the focus necessary to ignite others. This only comes from the God-given love: Agape. This is unconditional. Even when you do not want to, there is something on the inside of you that pushes you to display the love and character of Christ.

Secondly, people do not like imposters or people who are not genuine. They know when you mean it and when you do not. They know when you are putting on and doing things just to be seen by others. They generally can sense when there is an ulterior motive or hidden agenda. Be real. Be genuine!

Finally, one of the most challenging things to do is to be consistent. Excited one week and discouraged the next; fully engaged for two weeks and disinterested the next week; speak and hug you one week and avoid you the next week! If you are going to be effective in your influence and in igniting those around you, be consistent! If you are going to love, love hard! If you going to support, always be found supporting. *Vision Enhancers understand that their ability to serve and ignite others is not circumstantial; it has become their lifestyle.*

3. Echo the Voice of the Leader

An effective Vision Enhancer gains a clear understanding of the vision and the heart of their leader, then desires to echo it to all of those that are serving! Paul says in 1 Cor. 1:10, "Now I beseech you, brethren, by the name of our Lord Jesus Christ, that ye all speak the same thing, and *that* there be no divisions among you; but *that* ye be perfectly joined together in the same mind and in the same judgment." One of the greatest frustrations of any leader is to lend their heart and voice to their people for clarity, only to have those individuals leave and not fully embrace all that's been shared. This occurs because the people do not sound like their leader and are not speaking the same thing as their leader. The Pastor says that we are headed right and moving in this direction and everyone has questions. "Why does the Pastor want to go right? I think we should go left. I just don't understand why he is doing things like this." Having no one to echo their voice, or run with the vision, or encourage unity amongst the body can literally drain the strength of your leader. *Vision Enhancers understand that their voice carries significant weight.*

A Vision Enhancer says things like this:

- "Considering the vision of our church, it would probably be best to_____"
- "Knowing the heart of our Pastor, we should_____"

- "According what was outlined by our leader, we should probably_____"

I know you might be reading this and saying, "This seems silly." Others might think that this is being a suck-up to the Pastor, but you are doing something spiritual by coming into alignment with what God desires for the ministry and echoing the voice of your leader.

As a Vision Enhancer, you understand that you begin to refresh your leader when you echo their voice! Your leader should never have to toot their own horn. Your leadership should never have to seem to be self-propagating. For instance, I have witnessed some leaders standing to request that the church do something special to honor them for appreciation or church anniversaries simply because they did not have anyone who understood their voice in support of their leader. It is not your leader's role to mount the pulpit and encourage the people to celebrate him, or to bless him with monetary gifts or words of encouragement. This is out of order! Why has God placed you there? This is where the Vision Enhancer has the ear to hear the voice, embrace the vision, and have the wisdom necessary to translate it to others.

Handles Being in the Background

We live in a time now where everyone wants the lime-light and popularity! Everyone wants the camera, stage, lights, and all the public recognition that comes with it. But when God calls you to serve the vision of your leader, this cannot be your motivation. The life of the Vision Enhancer is often an assignment that requires one to serve without being seen.

The Vision Enhancer's role is to support their leader in such a way that it creates a culture of victory for everyone!

In Exodus 17, the Israelites are in battle with the Amalekites and are seeking to gain victory. Moses goes to the top of the hill with his staff in his hand, and he must keep his hands lifted for Israel to prevail. When his hands lowered, the Israelites would begin to lose and the Amalekites would start winning. Moses discovered that he could not do this alone. He needed the support of two individuals (the Vision Enhancers-Aaron and Hur) to keep his hands lifted so that victory could be gained for all of Israel.

We learn some essential lessons from this passage of scripture. This story unlocks some supernatural principles when it comes to supporting leadership. The Israelites could have easily shifted their focus and placed Aaron and Hur on the battlefield and told them to help fight. But they understood that victory was not going to be won on the ground level fighting in the natural, but rather when they came together and fought to keep their leader's hands lifted!

God did not place you at your ministry or in your leader's life just to sit. He placed you there so that you could be a source of refreshing and strength to the overall vision. Your role is to ensure that your leader is not growing faint, to make sure that you are there to support the vision, and to discern when the leaders are growing weary. The victory of your ministry and the fulfilment of the vision really rests in the strength of your leader. If they are worn out doing the menial task and work, they never can be released to do what God really has called them to do. Acts 6:2 tell us, "Then the twelve called the multitude of the disciples unto them, and said, It is not reasonable that we should leave the word of God, and serve tables." When you keep your leader's hands lifted by being a significant support in your given area, he is released to function in the grace to which God has called him, and a cloud of victory will remain in the house!

The Reality of the Background

One of the things that you will soon discover is the power of Vision Enhancer's ability to serve and never be seen! You are probably asking, "Well, what do you mean?" These are individuals who make a major impact in the lives of their leaders and on the vision, but are never brought to the stage for everyone to know who they are.

I will never forget my opportunity to visit one of my favorite mega-ministries that I watched on television. It was an experience for me because I got the opportunity to not only visit one of their services, but also to speak with a few of their ministry staff members. They walked me around to various parts of the ministry and showed me how it all went down, from their media center with cameras, to sound engineers, to the individuals who created marketing materials. I got the chance to shake the hand of the person who led the team that created media concepts and the marketing of messages, fliers, events, and more. I was amazed because I admired the Pastor's excellence and ability to birth creative concepts, but it never dawned on me that he was not the brain behind all the development! This man of short-stature was never on stage; he was never brought out and recognized or even acknowledged publicly, but he has made an enormous impact on the effectiveness of the leader's marketing and evangelism to the world!

So, what am I saying?! *You must have the heart to serve your leader without a spotlight.* You might have major impact on the ministry by guiding some of the financial processes and ensuring that you position the church to be effective in budgeting and fiscal stability; perhaps you might be writing the curriculum for the Christian Education of the ministry, providing everyone with excellent courses and training that strengthen the biblical knowledge base of the church; you might be armor-bearing your Pastor and have to take him to ministry engagements and ensure they have everything needed to fulfil their ministry assignments. All of this might be done behind the scenes, but all of it is necessary for the functionality of the overall vision. Nobody knows the sacrifice, labor, and countless hours spent doing what you do! *The Vision Enhancer does their greatest work when the cameras are off; this is where their true dedication is discovered.*

If you are going to be effective in handling the background, you must understand the following things.

1. <u>Check Your Motives</u>

When serving in various areas, you must often return to the question, "Why am I doing what I am doing?" Yeah, WHY? Why be a part of the leadership team? Are you on the team because you feel it's going to put you closer to your leader? Are you on the leadership team so that your leader can use you more and have you on the microphone out front preaching, teaching, or exhorting? You might have to ask yourself, "Why am I heading the Anniversary committee?" Is it to boss people around and show them that you know what you are doing? Is it for you to be recognized at the end of it with a plaque as the best committee chair in the history of the church? Are you trying to outdo someone else? Are you competing?

The Vision Enhancer must constantly check the motive of his heart to ensure that he has the proper motivation while serving. Your prayer must constantly be like David's, where you are asking the Lord to create in you a clean heart and renew the right Spirit (Psalms 51:10).

2. Humble Yourself

As a Vision Enhancer, there will be areas where your skill set or abilities might be greater than your leader. For example, your leader might not be able to sing or even hold a note. You are serving as the Praise and Worship leader and are responsible for leading the people into worship on a weekly basis. Just because your leader does not sing, does not mean you have the right to get a big head! "My Pastor can't tell me anything about music because this is my expertise." *Your leader might not have your expertise, but they have the Holy Spirit that gives them insights on how to provide oversight for the vision.*

Just because God is using you in a certain area does not release you to be unteachable! You must remain humble. Open. Pliable. Teachable. 1 Peter 5:6 tells us to "Humble yourselves…." That's right, it is something that you must do yourself. Nobody should have to get you in line or check you. The Vision Enhancer knows when they are feeling themselves; they know when they are becoming haughty and arrogant; they know when they are "smelling" themselves. The Holy Spirit will bring about a conviction that causes realignment. This is when Vision Enhancers humble themselves under the mighty hand of God and allow God to make them pliable so that they can continue to be used for His glory! Remember that God did not call you to be the Pastor (or at least, in this instance). I am not concerned with how well you administrate, operate, or delegate, you are still not your leader. Humble yourself! This allows God to continue to use you and grace you to fulfill the assignment, enhance the vision, and bring glory to God!

3. Never Toot Your Own Horn

One of the most rewarding things to see is the fruit of your labor. You might have worked tirelessly decorating the church for an event or function. Everyone comes in and admires the excellence and how things look, not knowing that you spent your entire weekend making sure things were in place. Some of you like it to be known that you were the one behind the success. NO! *A Vision Enhancer never reads their own accolades or brings attention to themselves.* You are saying, "Yep, this was all me! These candles, lighting, tables, and décor...yep, I did all this!" You are telling people, "Shoot...I stayed up here until almost one o'clock in the morning making sure all of this was done...I'm tired!"

A Vision Enhancer loves to bring honor upon their leader/ministry and bring Glory to God, not themselves. It ought to really bring you joy when you know that people are being blessed by what you are doing. *You celebrate on the inside when your leader shines!* You understand that it's not about you, but it is rewarding to see the vision coming to pass and knowing that God used your hands to further its fulfillment! Stop feeling the need to toot your own horn. Learn how to embrace the background and the blessing of being able to serve.

Remains Cutting-Edge

Lastly, the role of the Vision Enhancer is very important because they ultimately affect the functionality of the overall vision. Your goal is to become a vital asset to your leader/ministry and to add great value by serving with significance. A leader does not need just anyone around them, but they need individuals that are sharp, cutting-edge, and innovative. They have taken the time to understand the vision and the heart of their leader, spent time developing ideas, and formulating strategies that will progress the areas in which they serve.

Versatile and Adaptable to Change

A Vision Enhancer understands that God is a God of progression and change. Although He is the same God with the same character yesterday and forever more, His methodology and movements often change. It is the same with ministry. The focus of all ministries should be a message centered on the gospel of Jesus Christ, but the method often evolves. What worked at your ministry in the 1970's probably is no longer relevant and effective today. The style of reaching teens in the 80's is much different than reaching teens in this day and age. A Vision Enhancer understands that, in order to be effective within the area and in the capacity served, you have to be open to change. Your leader might have you doing something a certain way for a few months and then make adjustments to its direction. He might sense the moving of the Holy Spirit and totally reconstruct the area where you became comfortable. And if you are stuck in position, power, and placement you will have a difficult time going with the flow of the vision.

The Vision Enhancer knows that placement is never permanent.

Never get so caught up and glued to the place where you serve that you are unable to adapt to necessary changes. **You have to love the vision more than you love your assignment.** So, if that means you must be moved, be shifted, be realigned, or make changes within the area that you serve, then your heart is open and pliable to do it without resistance. Ultimately, it's all about the fulfillment of what God desires to do through the vision, and you are simply being used as a vessel in serving.

1 Chronicles 12 talks about David's mighty men, who were assigned to assist him. One of their characteristics found in verse 2 was that they were ambidextrous; they could use both hands when shooting arrows. They were skilled! This meant they were not limited to one way of doing things. Depending on the situations, these men might have needed to switch to using the other hand. They had enough skill to effectively make the switch without experiencing a decrease in effectiveness. Your leader needs people around him that are spiritually versatile! A Vision Enhancer knows how to handle changes and is not shaken when things need to be adjusted, even at the last minute. They simply flow! You are a tremendous blessing to your leader when they know you will not catch an attitude, be shaken or thrown off, and that you possess the maturity needed to handle changes while serving the vision. *Vision Enhancers understand that vision is about serving the leaders vision and not necessarily your personal preference.*

Lovers of Knowledge

One of the great characteristics about a Vision Enhancer is that they are lovers of knowledge. They want to stay on top of their area and learn all they can about it. Hosea 4:6 says, "My People are destroyed for a lack of knowledge." You become a vital part of the vision when you become an expert and take time to master the area in which you serve. For example, if you are serving in fundraising and assisting your leader raising monies for various outreach efforts at your ministry, there will be some things that you need to know. What's the best avenues to fundraise for a ministry? What are examples of success stories of those who have raised large amounts with their effort? What are things that I should avoid ? What are things that I should do?

If you are serving in marketing team for your ministry, you will need to stay abreast of that area. Marketing is constantly upgrading and evolving. You need to discover ways to effectively get the message out. What are ways to most effectively gain the attention of your targeted demographic? What are effective ways to appeal to the Millennials?

There are three things that Vision Enhancers do to stay knowledgeable within the area that they serve:

1) *Read and utilize resources*

   You must read! Pick up resources at the bookstore and online that are going to strengthen your knowledge base. Refuse to become outdated, obsolete, and dull!

2) *Gain a model/example*

   You should find individuals who are doing it bigger and better than you. Refuse to compare yourself with those on the same level, but challenge yourself and model those who are doing more. Do not steal ideas, but be creative and implement similar strategies that fit the scope of the vision of where you serve. There are times when you are required to create something that does not exist yet, but other times we can implement strategies that are working for someone else.

3) *Change your Circle*

   Iron sharpens iron. To remain sharp and cutting-edge, you have to stay around people who are sharper than you, who know more than you, and who have more than you. This is the only way that you can expand on what you do. Being trapped in a box and thinking that you have the best thing going is a very quick way to lose your relevance. Often, when God wants to expand you and stretch your thinking, He will start with those in your circle.

Creative Innovation

Effective Vision Enhancers take time to not only gain the knowledge, but to develop and create. Most people who serve do not spend enough time developing strategies and therefore never implement them. It's going to take time. It will not happen overnight. You are there to see it, develop it, and create ways to enhance your leaders vision. A Vision Enhancer seeks to enhance things by developing the "3 E's" within their area of service:

1. *Efficiency*

   This means that you achieve maximum productivity with minimum wasted effort or expense. A Vision Enhancer really does an analysis of things that are functioning and working in their given area of serving.

They determine what is working and what's not; they identify where time is being wasted; they discover where energies can be allotted in other areas; they uncover how to better maximize ministry opportunities. Your role is to use innovation and strategies that promote and further the productivity of the efforts that surround the vision.

2. *Effectiveness*

The Vision Enhancer is driven by the effectiveness of their efforts. This is determined by how adequately you are producing a desired or intended result. This means creating and setting goals within a given timeframe and sitting down at the table to evaluate their effectiveness. Did you reach your financial goals? Did you gather more souls? Did this increase the cohesiveness of your team? What were the gains? Is what you are doing making a significant impact? Never "be a member" or take up space. Be impactful and effective in all areas!

3. *Enormous (thinking)*

The Vision Enhancer always thinks BIG! You might have had success in various areas but never settle at your last success. Your wins and successes should only motivate you to think of ways to do things bigger and better than before. Last year you might have been able to raise $5,000 for your event, but this year you set $10,000 as a goal. You might have been innovative and created youth programming that saw 100 kids per week last year, but you want to double the amount of youth served the following year. Yeah, that conference was good, but you always are finding ways to turn "good" into "great!" Vision Enhancers are passionate and never stop thinking of ways to take things to the next level!

4

PITFALLS OF A VISION ENHANCER

The enemy is never happy when you decide to become a Vision Enhancer. It is a threat to Satan's kingdom, because the agenda of the Kingdom of God is advancing through people who have submitted themselves to serve another man's vision and become a runner in the earth. There are some very common pitfalls and traps that the enemy sets to deter the Vision Enhancer from staying the course and remaining focused on the completed picture of vision fulfillment. I want to clearly outline common pitfalls that you will experience while serving, as well as the essential tools needed to maneuver around them.

Offense

How you ever been offended? Have you ever felt like you were treated unfairly? Have you ever been wronged by a person who you held dear to your heart? Well, if you haven't, keep living because the Bible says in Luke 17:1, "…It is impossible but that offenses will come…" This is probably one of the more common pitfalls that you will encounter when serving. It's the enemy's desire to stagnate you and cause you to never leave the sideline and engage in serving, or cause you to uproot and leave the place God called you to because of an offense. I want to provide you with the truth concerning offense and the strategies of the enemy that try to come to keep the Vision Enhancer bound.

What is Offense?

Offense comes from the Greek work, *Skandalon*. It literal meaning gives the illustration of the part of the trap on which the bait is hung to lure the animal into the trap. We must understand that offense is a trap used by the enemy to try to ensnare us. You must realize that you are not wrestling against flesh blood, but you are engaged in a spiritual fight with the enemy. It is his desire to trap the Vision Enhancer while serving their leader and working on the vision that God has set before them. He uses offense to magnify situations only to distract you. What does this look like practically?

Sources of Offense

There is an exhaustive list of ways that the enemy tries to offend the Vision Enhancer. I won't dare go down the whole list, but I'll give you (5) of the most common entryways of offense while serving. Be honest with yourself and discover how the enemy keeps trying to trap you with reasons to be offended.

1. *Not Getting Your Way:* Pastors often deal with doing things in the right timing. Your idea of timing might be different from the timeframe that God has given them. You might suggest an idea or put something on the table, but it might seem undervalued or overlooked. Your Pastor tells you, "Let's wait on that." Or, you are simply told, "No." You don't understand why and become offended.

2. *Communication Style of your Leader:* Your Pastor might have to communicate to you in a way that you don't deem necessary. They may not consider how the instructions are delivered and are solely focused on the assignment being carried out. You believe their tone, treatment, and body language were harsh or insensitive, and you become offended by their words or actions. You just believe that you and your leader can't seem to see eye-to-eye.

3. *Not Being Included:* There might be a committee, team, or group that is selected for a certain assignment. You are not selected to be a part of something that you feel that you should be a part of. You are not clear as to why you are not invited, selected, or asked to be involved.

4. *Not being Spoken to or Acknowledged:* You believe that people are so rude! You might attend a ministry and there are those individuals with whom you are constantly battling. It might be vocal or perhaps even silent! They walked by you and didn't speak. They saw you and ignored you. They are inconsistent with their ability to be genuinely kind toward you and you've

simply had enough. You feel that you don't have to take this type of treatment and it gives you the green-light to stop attending, serving, and functioning where God has called you to be. You are offended.

5. *Being Rejected:* You feel that you love, care, and look out for everyone else, but when you need someone to do the same for you, no one is there. Your leader or others at the ministry might have missed your birthday, didn't call and check on you when you were absent, didn't reach out to you when you were sick, showed no regard for your feelings, or seemingly always forget about you. You are offended and feel that your leader or ministry doesn't really care about you.

Once the enemy gains your attention with the bait, he lures you to that place and traps you with offense.

Signs of Offense:

Once the enemy lures you to the place of offense, there will be certain signs of your entrapment. These signs are often a confirmation that we have allowed the enemy to rob us of our focus. In turn, they limit our ability to effectively be the Vision Enhancer that God called us to be. Here are some of the signs of Offense:

- *Cold Love*: It is very challenging to display and give love when you are offended. When offenses settle in the heart, it prevents you from genuinely giving. You at one time loved your ministry and your leader and would do anything necessary to promote and serve the vision. Since the offense, it is hard to show your love, give it freely, and sincerely do what God has called you to do. It feels like a duty, task, job, and your heart for the ministry and your leader is leaving or has left.

- *Strained Relationships:* Be alarmed when your relationship with your leaders seems strained. It might feel like something is not the same... something isn't right; things aren't the way the used to be; things are simply different and feel funny. You never want your relationship with your leader to be strained, and it's your responsibility, as the one who is serving, to ensure you protect and guard the relationship. The Bible says a brother offended is harder to win than a strong city and contentions are like the bars of a castle (Proverbs 18:19).

- *Resistance to Authority*: When you first came to the ministry and started serving, you were on fire. Now you are becoming very cautious, analytical, and have lost your honor for your leader. Those offended will not respond to their leadership properly. There once was willingness and value, but now there is resistance to serving. The resistance may not be full-blown rebellion, but it is felt at sensitive times. (Proverbs 19:20; Hebrews 13:17)

- *Drifting from Placement*: Detachment is first detected in an attitude of distancing, withdrawing from the place of accountability, and taking on the mindset of individualism instead of team-oriented with a spirit of unity. You once were involved, engaged, and sitting up front, and now you are coming late, leaving early, not communicating, and are disengaged from the vision. There is now a clear drift in the wrong direction. (Proverbs 27:17; Psalms 1:1-3; 27:1-10; 1 John 2:19)

Steps to Remaining Offense-Free

It is the enemy's goal to have you bound by the Spirit of Offense. It is also his purpose to distract you from being a runner of the vision and to cause a disconnection between you and your leader. It is important that you move quickly and not allow offense to lodge in your heart. Offense turns into deeper problems: resentment, unforgiveness, bitterness, and hatred. Here are the steps to avoiding offense and releasing yourself to remain free:

1. *Acknowledge*—Be honest with yourself and admit that you have been offended. Refuse to be in denial. You will never confront the offense until you acknowledge it.

2. *Have the Conversation*—Many people practice avoidance or denial and never have a conversation. Be willing to go to the person you believe offended you. Share your heart and have humility to share and listen (Proverbs 27:5).

3. *Forgive & Love*—Refuse to harbor unforgiveness and be willing to let it go. Open your heart up to the Love of

God (Agape), which can't be displayed outside the Holy Spirit (Ephesians 4:15).

4. *Move Forward*—The enemy wants you to be stuck and quit at the place of the offense. Muster up enough faith to move beyond the offense and remain grounded in the place God called you to be, serving the vision of your leader.

Familiarity

As a Vision Enhancer, you might have the opportunity to work very closely with your leader and church. Not only do you get to see the ministry within the scope of Sunday morning service, but you also get to work behind the scenes in more casual environments where you get to see your leader from a perspective that is not in the pulpit. The disciples were faced with the very same challenge in their interactions with Jesus. They had been walking with Him for a while and were able to see Him preach, teach, and perform many miracles. They were also able to be around Jesus when the crowd left, and interacted with Him on a closer, more intimate level. Just imagine...they saw Jesus on the stage and off the stage; they got to eat and drink with Him; they got to sleep in the same quarters and see Jesus more personally. In Matthew 16:15, He posed a question to them saying, "Who do you say I am?" Jesus understood that they had seen Him in various walks of life and wanted to really see if they understood who they were walking with!

A Vision Enhancer understands that there is both a divine and human side to their Leader.

When serving up close to your leader, you will get to see their human side. You might be able to go to lunch and just talk about life; you might have the opportunity to go to a sports game; you're going to see them with they are tired, frustrated, upset, silly, happy, sad, and much more. This is their human side!! They are real people who have feelings and have lives outside of church as well!

Just because you are in a space where you get to see their human side, doesn't give you the right to devalue their divine nature!

A Pastor is a shepherd who seeks after God's heart and feeds the people with knowledge and understanding (Jeremiah 3:15).

This person is empowered by God to release the power of God in our lives. Your Pastor is not your "guy;" he is not your "dude;" he is not just "Joe Blow."

The Spirit of Familiarity comes to breed indifference and become the equalizer. I will never forget the time that I was talking with an assistant of a Pastor who I greatly honored. I explained to him my honor for his leader and how I had followed his ministry for years. The assistant went on to talk about how his leader is "okay," and how he visits his house all the time, and how he gets to see his leader outside of the pulpit. He talked about how he has heard his leader for all these years and how he is "used to" it. It amazed me how familiar his assistant had become with his leader and how much he lacked honor for the man he was serving. Although other people all around the country were being blessed, healed, and delivered, he just saw his leader as a mere "man."

Familiarity is a mindset that that results in the power of God being hindered from flowing through the leader to you. It's an Anointing Blocker!

In Mark 6:1-6, we are given the example of Jesus coming to his hometown. These were individuals that might have seen Jesus grow up or interacted with Him as a child. They said "that's just Jesus…. the Carpenter, Son of Mary." Now Jesus was highly sought after to perform miracles and change lives in other regions, but when He arrived in his hometown, the people could not receive that because they were too familiar. Verse 6 lets us know that He could not perform many mighty works or miracles there because of their unbelief.

The enemy wants you to believe that you know everything about your leader and that you have seen all there is to them. You can no longer relate to them spiritually, but you can only see them through the eyes of carnality. You have seen them in different aspects and now you are saying things like, "That's just Pastor," or, "I know him really well." Let me remind you that there is more to your leader than you think! Refuse to place them in the box of commonality and close yourself off to receiving from them what God has for you.

You must ask yourself the following questions:

- Do I see my leader as an equal to myself?
- Have I lost a sense of admiration, respect, and awe when I come into his presence?
- Do I honor my leader and position myself to receive wholeheartedly from him?
- Do I have the mindset that I feel I can do what they do or even do it better if I were in charge?

The Vision Enhancer must constantly check their heart to ensure that the Spirit of Familiarity has not crept in. If you have said "yes" to any of these questions you are a candidate who can operate in this spirit. You must return to the place of understanding your leader's divine side and position yourself in humility to receive again. They are more than just a "man" or a "woman;" they are God's Man!

Burnout

Have you ever experienced trying to serve when you were out of strength? Tired? Overwhelmed? Juggling so many things that nothing seemed to ever get done? The role of the Vision Enhancer is often challenged and confronted with the whole idea of being burned out.

The term "burnout" was coined in the '70s by Dr. Herbert Freudenberger. The term was taken from an analogy of a burned-out house: "If you have ever seen a building that has been burned out, you know it's a devastating sight... some bricks or concrete may be left; some outline of windows. Indeed, the outer shell may seem almost intact. Only if you venture inside will you be struck by the full force of the desolation."[1] Freudenberger says, like a burned out house, someone who's burnt out may not seem that way on the outside, but "their inner resources are consumed as if by fire, leaving a great emptiness inside."[2]

---

[1] Freudenberger, Herbert J & Richelson, Geraldine. (1980). *Burnout: The High Cost of Achievement*, Anchor Press.

[2] Ibid.

Understanding the Weight of Your Assignment

You must realize that the place where you serve has a great impact on the overall vision. Whether you are directly working with your leader, serving in the area of audio/video, teaching a class, driving the van…all of it, in some form or another, is a very significant part of the overall vision. With every assignment, there are levels of responsibility, oversight, and work. That's right, WORK! James 2:17 says, "Even so faith, if it hath not works, is dead, being alone."

With every assignment, there comes a weight or burden of
ministry.

One of my favorite New Testament examples of serving is found in Mark 2:1-12. In this chapter, we are met with a man who could not move his body; he was paralyzed. The man sought to get inside the house, because he knew that Jesus had the power to heal him. Notice, the man had vision (to see) and saw himself going inside of the house but he did not have the legs to go into the place he envisioned. The Bible says that there were four men who committed to carrying him and making sure that he got in. But there was a major problem: there was no access to get in the house because it was filled to capacity. His friends decided to carry him up and bring him in through the roof!

Now imagine having to not only carry a person, but having to carry them against gravity up into an elevated place! This is synonymous to the role of the Vision Enhancers. Your leader can see the vision where God has called them to be, but needs people around them who can carry the weight of the assignment. I can just picture the men carrying him—needing to ensure that they held him properly, making sure that they did not drop him, making a physical sacrifice to ensure that another man's vision was fulfilled, and ensuring that they made it in.

Your assignment is not easy! It's a very heavy thing. Having the responsibility of dealing with various people, being a leader, being the first to come and the last to leave, spending countless hours planning and strategizing, sometimes working and not seeing the any results, sacrificing your personal and family time doing the work of the ministry are difficult. These things can be overwhelming and with an improper understanding of how to serve effectively, they will ultimately lead to burnout.

<u>Seven Signs of Burnout</u>

1) *You lose your passion for the place you once loved*
   You must constantly check and assess your passion. Your passion is what drives you and what causes you to love the things that you do. One of the warning signs of burn-out is when you start to become dispassionate and dreading the places you once loved to serve.

2) *You are becoming task-oriented, not ministry-driven*
   An alarming sign of burnout is when you start being task-oriented. You start losing sight of ministry (serving) and start making it about all the task you have to complete. Never be governed or motivated by a paycheck or out of mere commitment; let your focus be about the overall vision, which is serving others.

3) *You move from a leader to a maintainer.*
   When God calls you to be a Vision Enhancer, you are not there to just maintain your area. This means it's not

prospering, you are just doing enough to get by, and you have lost the desire to develop and grow it into a significant part of the ministry. When burnout sets in, you are just clocking in and waiting for the time to clock out.

4) *You lose focus, clarity, and innovation*

When you become burned out you will often lose a sense of focus, clarity, and innovation. You no longer have the strength to plan and create strategy for innovation. Everything becomes blurry and your efficiency and effectiveness are waning. Losing sight of the vision is inevitable when burnout sets in.

5) *You drop the ball on accountability*

When individuals become burned out they start to lack in communication and accountability. People who are burned out will avoid interaction with their leader, shorten the communication and conversations, and begin to lack clarity and transparency. Things start to become grey.

6) *Your lack of patience with others*

Those in burnout lose their patience for all things pretty quickly. Things quickly will irritate you; you become easily frustrated; you no longer have the desire to deal with the people you have been called to serve. You cannot dislike people when they are the ones God has called you to serve.

7) *Your personal and family life is suffering*

Burnout has the potential to affect your personal and family affairs. You are no longer balancing and being an effective steward over your time. You often are overwhelmed and bringing ministry items home, along with your frustrations, and it is having a negative effect on other areas of your life. Your personal and family lives are being greatly impacted because of burnout.

How to Stay Refreshed While Serving

Now we all realize that burnout is real. It is one of the pitfalls of serving effectively and of becoming a significant part of what God is doing through your leader's vision. So the question becomes: How do I avoid burnout? How do I stay refreshed? How do I maximize serving? Below are strategies and insights on how to stay refreshed!

1) *Recapture the vision and your calling.* One of the first things that you should do when you become burned out is to rediscover why you are doing what you are doing. This involves going back and being refreshed on the vision of your leader and understanding that the vision is larger than YOU! God has called you to serve, but not just to serve any kind of way. Not serving with a chip on your shoulder; not serving coming in tired and worn out; not serving like you are doing someone a favor, but serving with a heart of humility and with the focus of serving people. Do not allow yourself to drift or to get swallowed up in the work of the ministry. Whatever capacity you are serving in, understand that God will get the glory and you will have a strong impact on the furtherance of the vision.

2) *Input Determines Output.* One of the biggest challenges of serving is finding time to fill up after pouring out. When you are a Vision Enhancer your

primary role is to give, give, give. Give your time, talent, treasure, ideas, concepts, strategies, energies, and much more. You are constantly giving out. So, when do you have time to receive and fill up? You must find time to refresh your with God's Word, by reading the Bible. You must set aside times to pray and intercede for your leader and for God to continue to grace you for the assignment. You must know when you are running close to empty and take time to yourself privately to cleanse your lens and perspective. You might have to shut down all ministry work by a certain time, set standards where you have family time and avoid compromising it with any work, or go out of town or do things that you enjoy outside of serving. If you keep giving out and never take time to refresh, you will find yourself always burned out and ineffective in the place that God called you. You must know yourself and know what it takes to keep you refreshed, avoiding emptiness!

3) ***Cast Not Carry.*** In the beginning of this section we talked about the burden or weight of the ministry. The larger the vison, the heavier the weight of the assignment. You will feel it! But God promised us that

He would never put more on us than what we could bear. God gives us the perfect remedy when it comes to what we should be carrying. 1 Peter 5:7 says, "Cast all your cares upon me for I careth for you." When the load gets too heavy and you do not have all the answers, give it God! When you have done all, you can and do not know what else to do, do not continue to carry it, but cast it to the One who can give you everything that you need. The vision is too large for you to accomplish alone. You will never be able to effectively serve and be a blessing to your leader in your own strength. Your strength will run out! That's when God assures us that His strength is perfected in our weakness (2 Cor. 12:9)! This means that when you run out, God is obligated to give you more. Some of you might be saying, "I cannot go any further." But that's when God kicks in and becomes your strength. *The key to being a Vision Enhancer is understanding that naturally you have limitations, but supernaturally there are no limits or boundaries.* When your resources run out, He promised to give seed to the sower and to supply all of your need (2 Corinthians 9:10; Philippians 4:19). Tap into God's supply and you will never run out and always stay refreshed!

4) *Honor the Sabbath.* God was so wise that even He knew the importance of the Sabbath; on the seventh day, He rested (Genesis 2:3). Although some might debate over which day is really the Sabbath, the important lesson is to understand the value of rest. You need time to get away from everything and simply rest. Those who are highly successful will explain to you that they work tremendously hard planning, creating strategy, innovating, having meeting, events, etc. But they will also tell you that one of the keys to their success is understanding when to rest and learning to value those times. Some of you reading this book need a vacation—a real getaway—time to just rest and relax. Put work down for a brief stint, only to pick it back up with fresh new strength, vitality, insight, passion and perspective!

Improper Relationships

When God calls you to serve your leader and become a Vision Enhancer, it requires an alignment with the sacrifices of the assignment. One of the sacrifices that many individuals do not embrace is the understanding of how to effectively delegate relationships while serving. 2 Tim 2:4 says, "Soldiers don't get tied up in the affairs of civilian life, for then they cannot please the officer who enlisted them (NIV)." When God called you to come alongside the vision and serve, you enlisted your life to be a Vision Enhancer. This also holds true in today's military; their standards, assignments, tasks, and a culture that exists once you enlist. There is an overall vision and goal set forth, and the enlistee's purpose aligns with fulfilling the given assignment.

Vision Enhancers are submitted to God, and their desire is to please Him. They are also accountable to their Pastor/leader in the earth. There are some distinct differences between the life of a solider and that of a civilian. Next, I want to provide you with insights on your assignment as a Vision Enhancer and ways not to get entangled with relationships that will disrupt your effectiveness while serving.

Lack of Understanding

Some of the first things you must settle are the opinions of those who do not fully understand your assignment. These are people who might not attend church and just look from afar at the things you do for ministry or your leader. To them, it makes no sense that you dedicate all this time at the church. They might not be saved and really do not understand your dedication and commitment to seeing the vision advanced. They only witness you giving your time, talent, and treasure and they really cannot comprehend why you are doing *so* much. They are civilians! The disciples were also faced with this reality when their lives were totally transformed by their encounter with Jesus. In one account in the gospel of Luke, they are fishing and had left their occupations, as they knew them, to follow Jesus. This meant they left what was familiar and shifted their assignments from traditional fishermen to fisherman of men.

If you are going to be an effective Vision Enhancer, you must be willing to let go of the opinions of those closest to you.

You will hear all kinds of stuff! "So, you're down at that church again? You're giving them all your time? When are you going to do something for yourself? I don't think it takes all that!" If there is any doubt in your mind concerning why you are doing what you are doing, it creates a war within. You must know that God has called you and positioned both you and the purpose behind what you are doing. This understanding settles the war within so that you are not conflicted on what God has called you to do. Do not look for those on the outside to understand what God is doing. 1 Cor. 2:14 says, "But the natural man receiveth not the things of the Spirit of God: for they are foolishness unto him: neither can he know *them*, because they are spiritually discerned."

You will also have those on the inside who might not fully understand your assignment. There will be those who are merely members. Typically, these are the ones who try to provide the most commentary! They only come to church on Sundays and do not want to do anything else. They are consumers seeking to gain and receive everything that the church is giving out. They never position or humble themselves to be disciplined, which would activate them to give and serve beyond Sunday mornings. You must come to terms with it; *Everyone does not have a heart for the vision.* Everyone is not passionate about souls being saved, impacted, and touched, or about getting behind their leader to support the vision that God has given them. Vision Enhancers stay focused on the assignment and do not allow the opinions of others to become their reality.

Unequally Yoked

One of the pitfalls of the assignment is being in relationships with those where there is not agreement. Amos 2:2 says, "How can two walk together except they agree?" You may not realize it, but this has a significant effect on you and can become a great weight when trying to fulfill the assignment. Paul discusses this in 2 Corinthians 6:14: "Be ye not unequally yoked together with unbelievers…" A yoke is a wooden bar that joins two oxen to each other and to the burden they pull. An "unequally yoked" team has one stronger ox and one weaker, or one taller and one shorter. The weaker or shorter ox would walk more slowly than the taller, stronger one, causing the load to go around in circles. When oxen are unequally yoked, they cannot perform the task set before them. Instead of working together, they are at odds with one another.

Therefore, our relationships are extremely vital! You must ask yourself, "To whom am I connected?" Your connections will either cause you advancement in the things that God has called you do, or they will cause you much headache and to go in circles, being unproductive. Everybody is not supposed to walk with you in your assignment to be a Vision Enhancer. Soldiers have no business always hanging around civilians! There is something that God has placed on you to do, and if you surround yourself with the wrong people they begin to impede your effectiveness. You must accept that everyone who started with you will not be able to finish with you. They might have been able to handle you when you were just a member and unconcerned about vision, but now that you have awakened to whom God has called you to be, they can no longer walk on that level of assignment. And it does not mean that they are bad people; it does not mean that they do not love God; it does not mean that God is not doing something through them. But if God is going to get glory out of what you are doing, you must be spiritual enough to discern those who are fuelers and those who are drainers. You must surround yourself with people who are like-minded—those who are passionate about the vision, who understand the role of sacrifice, and who are willing to serve the vision and to make it happen for someone besides themselves.

Who to Talk to?

Being a Vision Enhancer can be somewhat of a lonely place. Everyone will not understand the weight of your assignment or the shoes you walk in. There will be times when you are serving and it seems like you have no one to talk to. This will especially occur at times when you need to just simply talk to someone and relate in conversation about serving your leader. Who will understand me? Who will be able to vibe with me and know my heart? Who will be able to keep what I say in context and not judge me? *A major pitfall of a Vision Enhancer is talking to the wrong people about things they shouldn't be exposed to.* Here are a few essential keys to keep in mind when determining your conversations and interactions:

1. Do not dump on those who are not connected to the Vision.

There will be times when you might come home after a long day or are simply overwhelmed and just want to talk to someone. You might have things that you are working on for the ministry or there may be a major event you are planning. These are times when we are most vulnerable to just dump our thoughts, concerns, or cares upon anyone who will listen. But you have to remember that you are a solider and not a civilian! You are on assignment for God and have committed to support the vision of your leader. Therefore, those who are not connected to the vision should not be given internal information about the inner workings of the ministry. Although they might be a good listening ear, those who are not connected to the heart of the vision are not likely to fully understand the context of the conversation. They have not labored like you have; they do not know the various dynamics of what is going on; they do not know the history or level of investment. **Often when we dump on people who are not connected to the vision or who are our family members, it can be a hindrance for them to totally receive or connect to the place where you are.**

I will never forget speaking with the spouse of a leader at my former ministry. I could never understand why her husband would not come and be a consistent member of the church or get activated in any area of ministry. I had the opportunity to speak with him one week and I asked him the reasons for his reservations and not being totally committed to the church. He surprisingly explained to me some of the conversations with his spouse and how he never wanted to take part in something that required that much stress. His spouse would come home and dump everything upon him, when he did not have the maturity or perspective to understand the place where she served. Although it was not necessarily negative things, it reflected the weight of the assignment and as a person who cared for her, he did not want to witness that level of pressure first hand.

This taught me such a valuable lesson. People who are not connected to the vision will not understand your level of serving and cannot be used as a mere sounding board when we feel the need to talk. This can be more of a stumbling block to them and can hinder them from fully submitting or supporting the vision of your leader/church.

Vertical and Horizontal Conversations

Leaders talk with Leaders! *Vision Enhancers talk to Vision Enhancers!* Many make the mistake of needing to just talk with someone and talk to the wrong people. You are serving in an entrusted area, whether that's in direction interaction with your leader or in a key area of the vision. You cannot afford to talk to the wrong people!

Some make the mistake of having casual conversations with those whom they are leading. This is a major pitfall of the Vision Enhancer. If you are the leader of the culinary team and have individuals serving under you, these are not the people with whom you should be sharing your frustrations, concerns, or stresses. They are looking to you to be the infuser of the vision and translating it to them so they can continue to have clarity and passion when serving. *If you contaminate them with your temporary feelings, it will hinder the long-term results of the vision.* You cannot share everything that you know; you cannot share everything that you see; you cannot share everything you feel.

When you hit places in ministry where you need to have helpful conversations, there are certain people you should enlist. First, there is need to seek God and His counsel.

Then when relating to people, there are two levels on which you should share:

1. Horizontally

This means you talk with individuals who share your same capacity for serving. They might be leaders within the same or similar area. These are individuals who share some of the same struggles, stresses, and experiences while serving the vision. They can totally understand, they can vibe with you, and they have the maturity to properly compartmentalize the things that you share. There always are individuals who are committed to being a Vision Enhancer who can provide the necessary encouragement and insight to keep you on the road of serving with significance. These are not people that are going to tell you to stop serving, or to quit being faithful, or to go somewhere else, or to disconnect from your leader. They have had similar struggles and know what it means to be planted in faithfulness to the assignment that God has called you to!

After speaking with them you feel better, you find yourself refreshed, and you are motivated with fresh insights on how to serve more effectively.

2. Vertically

These are individuals who are in a leadership positions or who have been successful serving where you are. It is important to have individuals in this category who you can speak with so that you avoid bleeding on people you are leading, or on those not connected to the vision. Before you negatively affect those in the sphere of your influence, seek those on a vertical level who have the power to provide counsel and to support and pull you up! It is totally illegal to be in backroom meetings and come out and share information and thoughts with those who are not allowed in that space. You eventually lose the honor and respect of those who serve under you, and you end up dumping a weight on them that they are not mature enough to handle. You ruin the culture in your sphere and never get the support needed to continue to serve in a place of excellence.

Before you start dumping on those who serve under you, have conversations with those in leadership. If your Pastor is accessible, reach out and have a conversation with him. At all costs, avoid bleeding on those whom you are called to influence!

5

THE BLESSING OF A VISION ENHANCER

Throughout this book, we have examined the Vision Enhancer and the characteristics needed to be effective in your given area of service. We have also considered the pitfalls and ramifications that can cause one to derail and lose sight of their assignment. In this chapter, I want to look at the some of the blessings that are attached to serving someone else's vision!

The motive of the Vision Enhancer is very important as it reveals the heart and intent behind what you do. I have witnessed individuals with impure and selfish motives which then become the focus and motivation behind their serving. Some serve to see what they can gain from it; other serve because they want to be next in line for the top spot; others serve because they merely want to be in the limelight and seen by others. These are examples of impure motives and do not reflect the heart that God desires us to have when serving others.

Serving should never be about what you can get, but about what you can give! Vision Enhancers never focus individually on what they can gain, but they think about what others will gain through their obedience in serving. Although the focus is not on YOU, the Vision Enhancer also understands that God honors serving and sacrifice! Many people use the scripture in Galatians 6:7, which says, "You reap what you sow…" in the context of negative behavior or wrongdoing. But this scripture also implies that if you have sown your time, sacrificed your life to ensure others were blessed, gave of your monies and resources, and done all you could to ensure someone else's vision was enhanced. God won't forget about you! Many of you have sown seeds for years and have had the heart of kindness and love, never to make things about yourself. Let me remind you, God has not forgotten about your labor of love! You have positioned yourself to reap a harvest of blessings that only God can unlock for those who have sacrificed their lives to bless others!

In this section, I want to highlight some of the experiences of two biblical men, David and Joseph, to provide further insight on the blessings attached to those who enhance the vision of others.

David's Experience

Blessing #1: Never Overlooked

Remember that David was a shepherd boy. His responsibility was to serve at his father Jesse's house by tending to all the duties pertaining to sheep. If you know anything about sheep herding, you know it is not the most highly desired job—it's dirty and tiresome. Some of you reading this chapter can also testify that the place where you serve might not be the most highly desired spot. It might come with cleaning up after people, being the first to come and last to leave, or dealing with people and things that no one else wants engage. It could mean being behind the scenes where no one else seems to value the things that you do. But consider David's job; it was highly necessary because it affected the overall livelihood of his family. It was a dirty job, but somebody had to do it!

In 1 Samuel 16:10-11, Samuel comes to the house looking for the next king, and all of Jesse's sons were presented—except David. David was not even considered and was left in the field, performing his day-to-day duties with the sheep. They did not think about him. They did not consider him. They did not view him as having the characteristics or outward appearance of a king. So instead of being noisy, pushing his way to the front, or even inquiring about what was going on in the front of the house, David remained faithful to his assignment and served this father's house with excellence!

When you have a heart, like David, to ensure that the house and vision of your leader is functioning well and with excellence, a special blessing is released over your life! You will never be overlooked! Let me say it again so that you can get this in the fibers of your Spirit: *YOU WILL NEVER BE OVERLOOKED!* The oil that was supposed to flow on the others did not flow and they could not be considered as the next king. However, when David was brought to the front, the oil that would not flow on the others flowed easily over his head! Never think that those who go before you or appear to be advancing more quickly than you will take *your* place. God has a spot reserved for the faithful! He has a blessing for the ones who serve with the right heart and who are not motivated by the limelight! I heard someone say once that God will take you from the background to the forefront—from OVERLOOKED to OVERBOOKED! Never strive for position or toot your own horn! God graces the Vision Enhancer to have a life that's never overlooked, but a life where people get to witness God's favor that allows them to always rise to the top!

Blessing #2: Divine Opportunities

There are a lot of people out there merely seeking opportunities. These folks are called opportunists. These are people who do things with the agenda of having opportunities presented to them in return: "I'll scratch your back if you scratch mine, if you invite me, I'll invite you; if you like me, I can get them to like me as well!" Opportunists! The Vision Enhancer never seeks opportunity from the things they do while serving their leader. If there was nothing "in it for them," they would still be there to support and serve.

Although the Vision Enhancer does not seek opportunities when serving; opportunities inevitably will arise! You position yourself to be setup for opportunities, blessings, and favor that could not be unlocked unless you were in the posture of serving! Look at David's life! In 1 Sam. 17:17, his father wanted him to go down and take lunch to his brothers. Remember these were the same brothers that overlooked him, counted him out, and only thought he was good enough to play second fiddle to them. David decided to stay humble, submit to his father's request, and bring them lunch. Upon his arrival, he was introduced to a major problem: Goliath!

Vision Enhancers unlock divine opportunities because they have committed themselves to being an answer to someone else's problem!

The opportunity would have never been presented if David had not possessed the humility to follow the instructions of his father and be a blessing to his brothers. He was chosen to fight against Goliath, and he used his skill set, which included tending sheep, as confirmation of his abilities.

Often, God is using the things you deem insignificant as the very things that set you up for some of the largest blessings in your life! Some of you might not really understand why the Lord has placed you in the position in which you serve. You might deem it insignificant or a place of little value, not really understanding its greater purpose. Do you realize, God could have you sweeping the floors and cleaning the bathroom of the church one day, and bless you with a contract to clean hundreds the next? God can take you from being faithful to teaching 10 youth each week at Sunday School to overseeing a grant that sees hundreds of kids each week! Never see what you do as miniscule. When you have the heart to be faithful and serve your leader/ministry, God will open divine opportunities that will literally blow your mind! Do not try to make it happen yourself; stay positioned and God will cause doors to swing open in your favor! *God, through your service to someone else, is building your spiritual résumé and qualifying you for the next major opportunity that will revolutionize your entire life!*

Joseph's Experience

Blessing #3: Unlocked Dreams

Let's look at the story of Joseph as an example. Joseph was a dreamer. He initially had a dream where he saw his brothers bowing down to him, which caused them to despise him and consequentially, he was sold into slavery. He went to Potiphar's house and became the second in command only to be sent to prison after being falsely accused of seducing Potiphar's wife. Joseph the dreamer was locked up, and it appeared as if all his dreams were never going to come to pass.

It is often the role of the enemy to get you to believe that your dreams and visions will never be a reality. Some of you might be reading this book and experiencing all types of warfare. Your life might not be reflective of the things God showed you. Some of you believe you should be further along in life than where you are right now; others are frustrated in the place where you are because your finances and resources are limited. Others simply feel stuck! It seems contradictory; you are not in the place that you dreamed you would be. This is a very real predicament. Most of you have reached this place when serving the vision of another person—serving when you were lacking—you did not have confidence; you did not have faith; you did not totally understand what God was doing.

Joseph was locked up! But God would use the principle of serving someone else and unlocking their dreams as the catalyst to Joseph's ultimate freedom. The chief butler and the chief baker of the king of Egypt offended their lord, the king of Egypt, who then had them thrown in prison with Joseph. There they both had dreams but no one to interpret them according to Genesis 40:1-7. The Lord gave Joseph the interpretation, and both came to pass. The butler kept his job, and the baker lost his head. Then the Pharaoh himself had a dream that all the magicians of Egypt could not interpret. God was about to take Joseph from rags to riches in one inspired moment. When the king learned of Joseph's ability to interpret dreams, he sent for him and asked if he could interpret his dreams. Joseph was ready.

Our ability to assist and unlock the dreams of others will be the key needed to unlock our own!

Joseph did not know how he was going to get out of prison. He could have been upset and ignored the requests of the butler and the baker. But even while he was in prison, God gave him the heart to serve someone else! He understood the power of being a Vision Enhancer by providing support and clarity to the dreams of others. When you take on the Spirit of humility and seek to serve others, God is obligated to provide clarity for you. You might be experiencing a season in your life where things are not clear for you; you might be praying about the next steps to take or the things to do next in life, but if you stop thinking about YOU and bless someone else, you ultimately find the solution. Unlocking dreams for someone else is your key to gaining access to the things God has promised you! Your support opens doors for your dreams to be supported! Never underestimate the power of unlocking and interpreting the dreams of others; these are the things that are guaranteed to bless your own life!

Blessing #4: Promotion

Everybody wants to know how to be promoted and how to advance in life. The Bible clearly outlines how to access this and tells us where promotion comes from, "For promotion cometh neither from the east, nor from the west, nor from the south. But God is the judge: he putteth down one, and setteth up another (Psalms 75: 6-7).

Joseph's promotion had truly come from God. Immediately, Joseph found himself promoted to a position of power, second only to Pharaoh. It's important to understand that Joseph had either been serving as a slave or as a prisoner for seventeen years after the time that his purpose was revealed and before it was fulfilled. You might be reading this book and feeling like your life is confined, limited, or you may even be feeling imprisoned by where God has you in your life. Many of you feel like you are seeing much of the same scenery in life and wanting something different for yourself. Imagine Joseph: he was probably tired of living as a prisoner with a great dreamer locked on the inside. What do you do when you know that God has more for you? Take the lessons from Joseph's life: he refused to abandon his assignment and he remained focused. Galatians 6:9 reminds us, "Let us not grow weary in well doing: for in due season we shall reap, if we faint not."

God has an amazing way of promoting you right where you are! Joseph life's gives a powerful reminder of how God does not need to make you the #1 man for you to possess His favor. All throughout Joseph's journey he was a blessed and favored 2nd man! God used him greatly and brought him into a place of power and authority without ever needing the title of "first"! This is a reminder to never seek position but to seek God's power. Everybody has not been called to the "first" position. And that's the whole idea of the Vision Enhancer: you can serve so well and be a blessing to your leader/church that God blesses and overflows you in the place that you serve. Never become position-driven. Keep the right Spirit and always remember that it's not about you. Watch how God uses everything that you have been through and everything that you have sacrificed to ultimately bless your life and lineage forever!

ABOUT THE AUTHOR

Dr. Matthew L. Nesbitt is a refreshing voice to the local church and an anointed gift to the Body of Christ. With a passion to equip and train leaders within the local church on effective vision enhancement, coupled with a strong revelatory and teaching anointing, his ministry provides practical strategies that mobilize local churches and provide strength to the runners of the vision. His powerful insight and solid knowledge base have led him to impact countless many through conferences, seminars, and workshops. His wisdom penetrates by strengthening senior leadership, while empowering and infusing leadership teams with the necessary knowledge that will assist them as they undergird their leaders.

Nesbitt, the founder of MLN Ministries, has been afforded the opportunity to travel the country ministering the gospel with much power and demonstration. In 2016, he completed his formal education, graduating with a Ph.D. from the University of Illinois at Urbana-Champaign. He currently resides in Los Angeles, California with his wife, Dr. LaTasha "Dr. Nes" Nesbitt, their son Kyler, and their daughter JayLon.

www.ingramcontent.com/pod-product-compliance
Lightning Source LLC
Chambersburg PA
CBHW071133090426
42736CB00012B/2109